There Ought to be a Law...

...Or should there be?

Catherine McGrew Jaime

Books by Catherine Jaime include:

A Brief Financial History of the United States
A Brief Look at Machiavelli and the Prince
A Celebration of Black History: Teaching through
    Timelines, Lapbooks, Mini Units, a Novel and more
A Conservative Primer on Govt. and Economics
Booker T. Washington and W.E.B. DuBois:
    Two Speeches and an Essay
Failure in Philadelphia?
Lapbooking through American Government
Pro-Life v. Pro-Death:
    Abortions & the Supreme Court
Rebuilding the Nation: Reconstruction Era Cartoons
    and other Illustrations
Rebuilding the Nation: Reconstruction Era
    Documents and Cartoons
Simply Put: A Study in Economics
Tales from the Troubled South: Civil Rights in
    Alabama
Understanding the U.S. Constitution
Understanding Presidential Elections
Understanding the Electoral College
U.S. Constitution Topical Study

Creative Learning Connection
Madison, AL 35758
www.CreativeLearningConnection.com

Table of Contents

"Among the natural rights of the colonists are these: First a right to life, secondly to liberty, and thirdly to property: together with the right to defend them in the best manner they can."

Samuel Adams
(1722 – 1803)
Patriot, Founding Father

Introduction

How many times have we said or heard "there ought to be a law"? But is that true in most of the cases we lament? Do we really want laws to regulate what used to be considered "common sense"? And more importantly, are all those potential laws and regulations even constitutional?

~^~^~

I spend much time every week helping highschoolers to gain a better understanding of the workings of the U.S. government, and the reality of economic principles. As I do, I often marvel at their level of understanding versus the lack of understanding I often run into elsewhere – both among teens and adults.

This little booklet is a simple look at topics that are too important to be constantly lost in boring textbooks and complicated lectures. Clearly this is not meant to be an exhaustive look, but rather a brief introduction.

It comes from the very basic belief that the U.S. Constitution was, and continues to be, the foundation of our government. Without such a firm foundation, our government is on very shaky ground.

A Good Law?

A good idea does not equal a good law.

Yes, we want people to wear seat belts, exercise, and eat certain types of foods over other foods. But how do any of those fall under the very short list of things that government should be regulating?

Hint: They don't!

"Government exists to protect us from each other. Where government has gone beyond its limits is in deciding to protect us from ourselves."

Ronald Reagan
(1911 – 2004)
U.S. President

~^~^~

"As government expands, liberty contracts."

Ronald Reagan

Proper Role of Government

One of the primary goals of government should be the protection of
individual rights, not the trampling of
those rights. We should look at each
act of government through this lens:
is it protecting or trampling individual
rights?

"A government big enough to give you everything you want is a government big enough to take from you everything you have."

Gerald R. Ford
(1913- 2006)
U.S. President

Cost of Government

One of the first things we should ask when anyone talks about the government doing anything (at the local, state, or federal level): "How much will it cost and who is going to pay for it?"

"Government is a trust, and the officers of the government are trustees. And both the trust and the trustees are created for the benefit of the people."

Henry Clay
(1777 – 1852)
U.S. Rep & Senator from Kentucky

How Big Is Too Big?

With government, big is not better. I believe, as our founders believed, that we need government to provide for our common defense and promote the general welfare (but not to guarantee it), and not much more.

In Article One of the Constitution, the framers went to great lengths to spell out the limits of the law- making portion of the federal government. They had little fear of giving the government too little power, but great concern of giving it too much.

"We the people of the United States, in order to form a more perfect union, establish justice, insure domestic tranquility, provide for the common defense, promote the general welfare, and secure the blessings of liberty to ourselves and our posterity, do ordain and establish this Constitution for the United States of America."

Preamble to the Constitution
(1787)

Foundations of Government

From our founding the Declaration of Independence and the Constitution have been, and should continue to be, the bedrock of our government, **not** the U.N., and not foreign laws or foreign ideas.

Corollary: The Constitution in general and the Bill of Rights in particular, were written to protect citizens from the government, not the other way around.

"We hold these truths to be self-evident, that all men are created equal, that **they are endowed by their Creator** with certain unalienable Rights, that among these are Life, Liberty and the pursuit of Happiness."

Declaration of Independence
(1776)

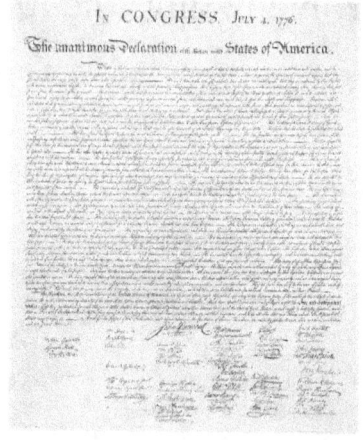

Separation of Church and State

A "wall of separation" between the church and the state is not in the constitution. The phrase was originally written by Thomas Jefferson in a letter to the Danbury Baptist Church in response to a letter they had written him. In Jefferson's letter, when he refers to the wall of separation, he was promising to protect the church from government, not government from the influence of religion.

So the current talk of "separation of church and state" is not only not what the first amendment says, it isn't what Jefferson said.

"I predict future happiness for Americans, if they can prevent the government from wasting the labors of the people under the pretense of taking care of them."

Thomas Jefferson
(1743 – 1826)
U.S. President

Pursuit of Happiness

The Declaration of Independence talks about the right to "life, liberty, and the **pursuit** of happiness" not "life, liberty, **and** happiness."

Contrary to what many people act like, government's role is **not** to give us happiness. And it will not succeed at something for which it has no constitutional mandate.

"I am for doing good to the poor, but...I think the best way of doing good to the poor, is not making them easy in poverty, but leading or driving them out of it. I observed...that the more public provisions were made for the poor, the less they provided for themselves, and of course became *poorer. And, on the contrary, the less was done for them, the more they did for themselves, and became richer.*"

Benjamin Franklin
(1706 – 1790)
Printer, Author, Founding Father

What is Compassion?

True compassion is giving people a hand up, not a handout. But even if we believed that handouts were really equal to compassion, where would the government get the authority to do give them?

We need to go back to the very important, and very basic, concept that the powers not specifically given to the federal government are reserved for the states and the people (see the Ninth and Tenth Amendments to the U.S. Constitution if that seems odd to you.)

To see the types of powers that are granted to the Federal Government, check out Article One, Section Eight of the Constitution. You may be surprised at how short the list is!

"And we can celebrate when we have a government that has earned back the trust of the people it serves...when we have a government that honors our Constitution and stands up for the values that have made America, America: economic freedom, individual liberty, and personal responsibility."

John Boehner
(1949 – present)
Congressman

Individual Responsibility

Just as we want the government to insure individual rights, we don't want it to interfere with individual responsibility. Our belief in individual responsibility goes deep – back to our Greco- Roman and Judeo-Christian roots.

We don't need (or want) government to tell us who to marry, or what job to take, nor do we need it to tell us how much school we need or how much food to eat. We need to be left alone to take responsibility for our own actions – including the risks and successes resulting from the choices we make.

"Those who manage their way into a crisis are not necessarily the right people to manage their way out of a crisis."

Albert Einstein
(1879 – 1955)
Scientist

Winners & Losers

Our government does not, and should not, exist to pick winners and losers. But that's what happens when "bailouts" and "stimulus plans" enter the government's budget.

Corollary: "No one is too big to fail." When the government bails out a company, for instance, the auto industry bailouts, the company can continue to make the same fiscally irresponsible decisions that got it in trouble in the first place.

"The first lesson of economics is scarcity. There is never enough of anything to satisfy all those who want it. The first lesson of politics is to disregard the first lesson of economics."

Thomas Sowell
(1930 – present)
Economist

Prices

In a free market, price is king! Or at least it is when the government doesn't interfere. But when the government places price ceilings (exa: gasoline prices after a hurricane), the predictable result is shortages. Conversely, when the government sets price floors, surplus is the necessary result. A prime example of that is when the government sets a minimum price at which labor can be sold (minimum wage), thereby setting a price floor. The predictable result is a surplus of labor.

"My reading of history convinces me that most bad government results from too much government."

Thomas Jefferson
(1743 – 1826)
U.S. President

Care vs. Insurance

Health Care is not the same thing as Health Insurance, though for several years the two terms have been used interchangeably. Everyone may need/desire access to good health care, but that does not equal the need for universal health insurance. Making health care truly affordable requires bringing the price down. But the price will only go down if the supply is increased. (Or if the government mandates lower prices – but like with other price ceilings that will cause a shortage instead!)

"I, however, place economy among the first and most important republican virtues, and public debt as the greatest of the dangers to be feared."

Thomas Jefferson
(1743 – 1826)
U.S. President

Mountains of Debt

When the federal government borrows money to pay for programs it cannot currently afford, it is stealing from future generations. A balanced budget would be one of the greatest gifts we could give to our children and grandchildren.

"The problem with socialism is that you eventually run out of other people's money."

Margaret Thatcher
(1925 – 2013)
British Prime Minister

What's a Fair Share?

"Rich" people already pay more taxes (and a higher percentage) than poor people. For those crying for them to pay their "fair share," I ask: at what point will they be considered to be paying their fair share? 60% 70% 80%? Even if we continue to raise the rates on the rich, there are not enough of "them" to fund all the government programs that people can imagine. What we're really accomplishing here is a simple "redistribution of wealth," and we should call it what it is.

"Government's view of the economy could be summed up in a few short phrases: If it moves, tax it. If it keeps moving, regulate it. And if it stops moving, subsidize it."

Ronald Reagan
(1911 – 2004)
U.S. President

Government as Robin Hood

Something "free" from the government is never really. Anything given away as "entitlement" has to first be taken from someone else.

If an individual took our money against our will, we would call it stealing, but when the government takes it by force, we call it taxes. But what's the real difference? (Yes, some taxes are necessary to run the government, but when it is actually the redistribution of wealth, there is nothing in the Constitution to support it.)

"An economy hampered by restrictive tax rates will never produce enough revenue to balance our budget, just as it will never produce enough jobs or enough profits."

John F. Kennedy
(1917 – 1963)
U.S. President

~^~^~

"The wise and correct course to follow in taxation and all other economic legislation is not to destroy those who have already secured success but to create conditions under which everyone will have a better chance to be successful."

Calvin Coolidge
(1872 – 1933)
U.S. President

Class Warfare

Class warfare has no place in the United States. We should not be talking about lower class and middle class as if we have some sort of caste society where people are stuck in one place or another. The terms "lower income" and "upper income" are much more meaningful.

In the U.S. people can move from one income level to another, and many will do exactly that over the course of their lifetimes. While it may not be the case in many other societies, here when we make less money than someone else, it should not cause envy, but rather rejoicing that we may someday have the opportunity to attain a higher income level as well.

"Incentive – nothing less than the interest one has in his own improvement – will mold the future just as surely as it shaped the past."

Lawrence W. Reed
(1953 – present)
Economist

Incentives

People react to incentives and disincentives. If we incentivize them to do something, we shouldn't act surprised when they do it!

Corollary: If incentives change, choices will change.

Example: When prices go up, we are incentivized to conserve, just as when prices go down, we are incentivized to use more of something.

"Ultimately property rights and personal rights are the same thing."

Calvin Coolidge

(1872 – 1933)

U.S. President

Property Rights

One of the most important concepts in economically-sound societies is the idea of property rights. If we don't own it, can we ever really build on it, improve it, or create with it? Where is our incentive if we don't have the rights to our own property?

In the early seventeenth century the Pilgrims tried a very brief and quite unsuccessful attempt at limiting property rights. Famine and hunger increased, rather than decreased, in this perfect example of "the tragedy of the commons." The solution was simple and effective: families were given their own plots of land, and the responsibilities and rights that went with them.

"The art of economics consists in looking not merely at the immediate but at the longer effects of any act or policy; it consists in tracing the consequences of that policy not merely for one group but for all groups."

Henry Hazlitt
(1894 – 1993)
Economist

Unintended Consequences

The long term effects of government policies seem seldom to be considered. We would also do well to consider what the "unintended consequences" may be.

For example, an unintended consequence of the "Cash for Clunkers" plan was to decrease the supply of used vehicles available for sale, raising prices on that scarce item, and hurting the very people the program claimed to aid – those in lower income brackets.

"We can erect walls to foreign trade and even discourage job- displacing innovation. Time and again through our history, we have discovered that attempting merely to preserve the comfortable features of the present-- rather than reaching for new levels of prosperity--is a sure path to stagnation."

Alan Greenspan
(1926 – present)
Chairman of the Federal Reserve

Outsourcing

How many people oppose outsourcing because it sends jobs overseas, but approve the idea of foreign aid? Outsourcing is the best form of foreign aid – helping a country through the power of the market.

And while it sounds good to say that as a country we should be independent, will that ever be the case? Or should we strive for interdependence?

"It is not from the benevolence of the butcher, the brewer, or the baker, that we expect our dinner, but from their regard to their own self-interest."

Adam Smith
(1723 – 1790)
Economist

"We have always known that heedless self-interest was bad morals; we now know that it is bad economics."

Franklin D. Roosevelt
(1882 – 1945)
U.S. President

Greed/Self Interest

Much is made of greed and self-interest, as if they are a bad thing. But do we really expect humans to act in any other way? Which of the previous quotes do you believe?

"In a truly great company profits and cash flow become like blood and water to a healthy body: They are absolutely essential for life but they are not the very point of life."

Jim Collins
Author

Profit

Along those lines, is making a profit a bad thing? If not, why is it so often demonized? If so, do we really expect companies to stay in business without making a profit?

Just as Adam Smith's baker and butcher have their own self- interest in mind while they conduct business, so do bigger companies. That is not evil, it is logical.

Only the market, through profits and losses, can efficiently lead a company to pursue innovation. When losses or insufficient profits occur, a company is motivated to pursue alternative methods or machines, find cheaper inventory, or discover other money saving options.

"The government is merely a servant -- merely a temporary servant; it cannot be its prerogative to determine what is right and what is wrong, and decide who is a patriot and who isn't. Its function is to obey orders, not originate them."

Mark Twain
(1835 – 1910)
Author

Conclusion

I hope this little booklet of quotes and thoughts on these important topics has made you think more deeply about your own ideas of economics and government.

I was influenced by studying many of our founders, including George Washington, the first president of the United States, who put it so well when he said: *"A primary object should be the education of our youth in the science of government. In a republic, what species of knowledge can be equally important? And what duty more pressing than communicating it to those who are to be the future guardians of the liberties of the country?"*

"Nothing is more certain than that the degree of economic progress of mankind will still...be commensurate with the degree of human knowledge."

Carl Menger
(1840 – 1921)
Austrian Economist

Article One, Section Eight
U.S. Constitution

The Congress shall have power to lay and collect taxes, duties, imposts and excises, to pay the debts and provide for the common defense and general welfare of the United States; but all duties, imposts and excises shall be uniform throughout the United States; To borrow money on the credit of the United States;

To regulate commerce with foreign nations, and among the several states, and with the Indian tribes;

To establish a uniform rule of naturalization, and uniform laws on the subject of bankruptcies throughout the United States;

To coin money, regulate the value thereof, and of foreign coin, and fix the standard of weights and measures;

To provide for the punishment of counterfeiting the securities and current coin of the United States;

To establish post offices and post roads;

To promote the progress of science and useful arts, by securing for limited times to authors and inventors the exclusive right to their respective writings and discoveries;

To constitute tribunals inferior to the Supreme Court;

To define and punish piracies and felonies committed on the high seas, and offenses against the law of nations;

To declare war, grant letters of marque and reprisal, and make rules concerning captures on land and water;

To raise and support armies, but no appropriation of money to that use shall be for a longer term than two years;

To provide and maintain a navy;

To make rules for the government and regulation of the land and naval forces;

To provide for calling forth the militia to execute the laws of the union, suppress insurrections and repel invasions;

To provide for organizing, arming, and disciplining, the militia, and for governing such part of them as may be employed in the service of the United States, reserving to the states respectively, the appointment of the officers, and the authority of training the militia according to the discipline prescribed by Congress;

To exercise exclusive legislation in all cases whatsoever, over such District (not exceeding ten miles square) as may, by cession of particular states, and the acceptance of Congress, become the seat of the government of the United States, and to exercise like authority over all places purchased by the consent of the legislature of the state in which the same shall be, for the erection of forts, magazines, arsenals, dockyards, and other needful buildings;–And

To make all laws which shall be necessary and proper for carrying into execution the foregoing powers, and all other powers vested by this Constitution in the government of the United States, or in any department or officer thereof.

Ninth & Tenth Amendments
U.S. Constitution

Ninth Amendment
The enumeration in the Constitution, of certain rights, shall not be construed to deny or disparage others retained by the people.

Tenth Amendment
The powers not delegated to the United States by the Constitution, nor prohibited by it to the states, are reserved to the states respectively, or to the people.

"It is not because men have made laws, that personality, liberty, and property exist. On the contrary, it is because personality, liberty, and property exist beforehand, that men make laws. Nature, or rather God, has bestowed upon every one of us the right to defend his person, his liberty, and his property..."

Frédéric Bastiat
(1801 – 1850)
French Economist

About the Author

Catherine Jaime did her undergraduate work at the Sloan School of Management at the Massachusetts Institute of Technology. She has taken additional economics training through the Foundation for Teaching Economics and the Foundation for Economic Education.

Catherine has taught high school economics and government. She has authored several books dealing with government and economics. She firmly believes in the importance of the U.S. Constitution and the free market, and it shows in her writings.